Littlefoot

Littlefoot

CHARLES WRIGHT

FARRAR, STRAUS AND GIROUX

NEW YORK

Farrar, Straus and Giroux
19 Union Square West, New York 10003

Grateful acknowledgment is made to the following magazines, in whose pages some of these sections first appeared: *American Scholar, Appalachian Heritage, Five Points, The Laurel Review, The New Yorker, Ploughshares, Poetry Northwest, Subtropics, Virginia Quarterly Review*, and *The Yale Review*.

Grateful acknowledgment is made for permission to reprint the following material:

"Will You Miss Me When I'm Gone" by A. P. Carter, copyright © 1935 by Peer International Corporation. Copyright renewed. International copyright secured. Used by permission. All rights reserved.

"Reunion in Heaven" by Earl Scruggs and Lester Flatt, copyright © 1955 by Peer International Corporation. Copyright renewed. International copyright secured. Used by permission. All rights reserved.

"Maple on the Hill" by Ralph Stanley, copyright © Zap Publishing Co., B.M.I. Used by permission.

Library of Congress Cataloging-in-Publication Data
Wright, Charles, 1935–
     Littlefoot / Charles Wright.— 1st ed.
        p.   cm.
     ISBN-13: 978-0-374-18966-2 (hardcover : alk. paper)
     ISBN-10: 0-374-18966-8 (hardcover : alk. paper)
     1. Mortality—Poetry.   2. Nature—Poetry.   3. Seasons—Poetry.   I. Title.
PS3573.R52 L57 2007
811'.54—dc22

                                                                    2006029980

Designed by Jonathan D. Lippincott

www.fsgbooks.com

1   3   5   7   9   10   8   6   4   2

*This book is for Robert Denham, of Emory, Virginia,
with gratitude and affection. "Alenda Lux . . ."*

Littlefoot

1

It may not be written in any book, but it is written—
You can't go back,
                        you can't repeat the unrepeatable.
No matter how fast you drive, or how hard the slide show
Of memory flicks and releases,
It's always some other place,
                              some other car in the driveway,
Someone unrecognizable about to open the door.

Nevertheless, like clouds in their nebulous patterns,
We tend to recongregate
                        in the exitless blue
And try to relive our absences.
What else have we got to do,
The children reamplified in a foreign country,
The wife retired,
                    the farm like a nesting fowl and far away?

Whatever it was I had to say, I've said it.
Time to pull up the tie stakes.
I remember the way the mimosa tree
                                    buttered the shade
Outside the basement bedroom, soaked in its yellow bristles.
I'll feed on that for a day or two.
I remember the way the hemlock hedge
                                    burned in the side light.

Time to pull up the tie stakes.
Time to repoint the brickwork and leave it all to the weather.

Time to forget the lost eyelids,

                    the poison machine,

Time to retime the timer.

One's friends lie in nursing homes,

                    their bones broken, their hearts askew.

Time to retrench and retool.

We're not here a lot longer than we are here, for sure.

Unlike coal, for instance, or star clots.

                    Or so we think.

And thus it behooves us all to windrow affection, and spare,

And not be negligent.

So that our hearts end up like diamonds, and not roots.

So that our disregard evaporates

                    as a part of speech.

———————

Cloud wisps, and wisps of clouds,

                    nine o'clock, a little mare's tail sky

Which night chill sucks up.

Sundown. Pink hoofprints above the Blue Ridge,

                    soft hoofprints.

If this were the end of it, if this were the end of everything,

How easily one could fold

Into the lapping and overlapping of darkness.

                    And then the dark after that.

———————

Saturday's hard-boiled, easy to crack.

                    Sunday is otherwise,

Amorphous and water-plugged.

Sunday's the poem without people, all disappeared

Before the shutter is snapped.

Rainy vistas, wet-windowed boulevards, empty entrances.

Across the bridge, dissolute, one-armed,

Monday stares through the viewfinder,
                              a black hood over its head.

———————————

When the rains blow, and the hurricane flies,
                              nobody has the right box
To fit the arisen in.
Out of the sopped earth, out of dank bones,
They seep in their watery strings
                              wherever the water goes.
Who knows when their wings will dry out, who knows their next knot?

———————————

In the affinity is the affection,
                              in the affection everything else
That matters, wind in the trees,
The silence above the wind, cloud-flat October sky,
And the silence above that.

The leaves of the maple tree,
                              scattered like Post-it notes
Across the lawn with messages we'll never understand,
Burn in their inarticulation,
As we in ours,
                    red fire, yellow fire.

It's all music, the master said, being much more than half right,
The disappearance of things
Adding the balance,
                    dark serenity of acceptance
Moving as water moves, inside itself and outside itself.

Compassion and cold comfort—
                              take one and let the other lie,
Remembering how the currents of the Adige

Shattered in sunlight,
Translucent on the near side,

                     spun gold on the other.

———————

Which heaven's the higher,

                  the one down here or the one up there?
Which blue is a bluer blue?
Bereft of meaning, the moon should know,

                  the silent, gossip-reflecting full moon.
But she doesn't, and no one descends to speak for her.
Time in its two worlds. No choice.

2

I am the sign, I am the letter.
I am the language that cannot be come to terms with.
I will go to my resting place
                    and will not be born again.
I am what is scattered and cannot be gathered up.
I am small, I am silence,
                    I am what is not found.

3

Moon like a hard drive
                            just over the understory
Freckling my neighbor's backyard,
Nightscreen unscrolling along the River of Heaven,
Celestial shorthand
Unasked for and undeletable
In time-lapse upon the early November skybook.

These are our last instructions,
                                of which we understand nothing.
The road map is there, the password,
                                    neither of which we understand.
They boil on our tongues like waterflies.
They cling to our fingers,
                         they settle along our still eyelids
As though we would succor them,
As though we could understand their wing-buzz and small teeth.

                 ————————

Wherever I've gone, the Holston River has stayed next to me,
Like a dream escaping
                     some time-flattened orifice
Once open in childhood, migrating now like a road
I've walked on unknowingly,
                         pink and oblivious,
Attended by fish and paving stones,
The bottom breaks like mountains it slithers out of, tongued and chilled.

The river is negative time,
                     always undoing itself,

Always behind where it once had been.
Memory's like that,
Current too deep, current too shallow,
Erasing and reinventing itself while the world
Stands still beside it just so,
                    not too short, not too tall.

There's no uncertainty about it, negative time,
No numbering.
        Like wind when it stops, like clouds that are here then not here,
It is the pure presence of absence.
November's last leaves fall down to it,
The angels, their wings remodeled beneath their raincoats,
Live in it,
            our lives repeat it, skipped heartbeats, clocks with one hand.

Out of the sallows and slick traces of Southwest Virginia,
From Saltville and Gate City, from Church Hill and New Hope,
The river remainders itself
                    and rises again
Out of its own depletion.
How little we know it, how little we really remember it.
How like our own blood it powers on,
                        out of sight, out of mind.

Outside of the church, no salvation,
St. Cyprian says.
Outside of nature, no transformation, I say,
                    no hope of return.

Like us, November doesn't know this,
Leaf ends curled up like untanned leather,
                    grass edges bleared back from emerald ease,
Light-loss diaphanous in the bare-backed and blitherless trees.

4

Well, the wings of time pass, the black wings,
And the light is not adumbrated,

                           or dampened down—
Like splendor, there is no end to it
Inside the imagination,

                   then inside of that,
Wind-beat, light of light, and even into the darkness.

5

November noon mist, gold coins of leaves
Glittering through it as though refracted by sunlight
Through rain shower,
                        radiant clusters, radiant change,

Mountains rehollowed and blotted out,
Car lights continuous rosary beads
                                both ways on the Interstate,
Evening already released out over the dark Atlantic.

These are the still days,
                        stillness being the metaphor
Out of which every grain is revealed
                                and is identified.
Finger me, Lord, and separate me to what I am.

———————

In nature there is no past or future,
                                no pronouns, no verbs.
Old knowledge, Slick, old deadlights.
Still, the tongue does not know this, the half-lit and dumb tongue—

Precision of frogs and grasses,
                        precision of words,
Each singular, each distinct,
The tongue tries to freeze-frame them as they are,
                                and offer them to us.

Now is precise but undefinable,
                        now is nonverbal,

No matter how hard we work it out.
Nuthatch or narwhal,
                    like petals, words drift in the air.

———————

Calamities covet us, wild grass will cover our bodies,
We read in the Book of Poverty.
Deliver us, blessed immaculata,
                    adorn our affections.

Language is luckless and limitless,
                              as nature is.
But nature is not sincere, nor is it insincere—
The language of landscape is mute and immaculate.

First character of the celestial alphabet, the full moon,
Is a period, and that is that.
No language above to aid us,
                    no word to the wise.

———————

I leave a blank for what I don't know,
                    four syllables, _____,
And what I will never know.
Thrones, and assisting angels, this is a comforting.

In Kingsport, looking across the valley toward Moccasin Gap
From Chestnut Ridge,
                    the winter-waxed trees
Are twiggy and long-fingery, fretting the woods-wind,

Whose songs, ghost songs, wind-lyrics from sixty years ago,
Float back and exhale—
                    I will twine with my mingles of raven black hair.
Will you miss me when I'm gone?

6

The winter leaves crumble between my hands,
                                        December leaves.
How is it we can't accept this, that all trees were holy once,
That all light is altar light,
And floods us, day by day, and bids us, the air sheet lightning around us,
To sit still and say nothing,
                        here under the latches of Paradise?

7

Sunset, line like a long tongue-lick above the Blue Ridge,
Mock orange, then tangerine, then blush.

                                               How ordinary, dog,
The rush-hour car lights down Locust Avenue like quartz crystals,
Backlit and foraging forth.
Streetlights gather the darkness to them,
Compassion an afterthought,

                               mercy no thought at all.

Moon down, darkness fixed and unmoving,
Stars bobbing like water lights,

                               three weeks to the winter solstice,
Wind drift and tack from the north,
Night like a distance one could row on,
Whose depths are an afterlife

                               almost, whose sea is remembered
As half-crossed, its wave spray like wind dust.

Good luck bamboo in three shoots in high-glaze south German
        brown vase,
Front yard like a windowpane
Into the anteroom of all things untouchable,
Cycladic ghost mask,

                          little Egyptian and Zuni overseers,
Choctaw and pre-Columbian artifacts arranged
Against the ruinous dark waters

                             outside the horizon.

Time is your mother in a blue dress.

When was it I first heard of the blank,
The salve of nothingness,
                              all its engendering attitude?
When was it I felt the liquid of absolution
And all its attendant emptiness
For the first time, and what it might mean?
Not young, I'd have to say,
                    remembering not one thing about either of them.

How early, however, I learned of their opposites.
Muscadines plump in their plenitude,
Lake waters lowing at night under frog call,
                              night wind in leaf-locked trees,
Splash of the fishing lure, whisper of paddle blade and canoe,
Clouds like slow-moving cattle
Across the tiny and synchronized tip of the moon.

To walk up the Y-shaped hill
                    from the commissary
(This was a government town)
In summer under the hardwoods and conifers
Was to know the extension of things,
                              the deep weight of the endlessness
Of childhood, deep, invisible weight,
Lake-sound and lake-song in high hum, the future in links and
      chains.

To lie under lake-wind in August,
                    under mountain laurel
And blue-green North Carolina sky,

Lunch over, campfire smoke-ends
       drifting out over water glints,
Was something like nothingness, perhaps, and its caress,
Crusader knights in their white tunics
        and red crosses
Like ghosts through the trees, but not enough.

Precious memories, how they linger,
      how they ever flood my soul,
In the stillness of the midnight,
      precious, sacred scenes unfold.

8

Good luck is a locked door,
> but the key's around somewhere.
Meanwhile, half-hidden under the thick staircase of memory,
One hears the footsteps go up and the footsteps go down.

As water mirrors the moon, the earth mirrors heaven,
Where things without shadows have shadows.
A lifetime isn't too much to pay
> for such a reflection.

9

Three years, the story goes, it took the great ship to appear
In silhouette from the shadows
                              hanging above Lake Garda
And dock at the small port of Riva,
The Hunter Gracchus carried upon a bier by two men
In black tunics with silver buttons
Up to a back room in the mayor's office
                              until it was time to return onboard

And circle the waters of the world.
Unable to set down on land,
                              unable to leave this world,
The story goes on, because of a wrong turn of the tiller
This side of the other shore,
Some inattention,
The great ship and the great body,
                              like lost love, languish and lip the earth,

Received sporadically, recognized everywhere,
The ship with its infinitely high masts,
                                        its sails in dark folds,
Cobalt and undulant rocking of lake swells and waves,
Long runners and smooth slatch of the seas,
Creek hiss and pond sway,
Landfall and landrise
                    like Compostela at land's end.

There is no end to longing.
There is no end to what touch sustains us,

winter woods
Deep in their brown study and torqued limbs,
Fish-scale grey of January sky,
Absence of saints on Sunday morning streets,
                                        the dark ship,
Dead leaves on the water, the muddy Rivanna and its muddy sides.

We all owe everything to those who preceded us,
Who, by the lightness of their footsteps,
Tap-danced our stories out, our techniques,
                                        who allowed us to say
Whatever it was we had to say.
God rest them all in their long robes and vanishing shoes.
God grant that our figures be elegant,
                                our footwork worthy.

Faith is a thing unfathomable,
Though it lisp at our fingertips,
                            though it wash our hands.
There is no body like the body of light,
                            but who will attain it?
Not us in our body bags,
Dark over dark, not us,
                    though love move the stars and set them to one side.

Sunlight like I beams through S. Zeno's west-facing doors,
As though one could walk there,
                            and up to the terraces
And gold lawns of the Queen of Heaven.
I remember the lake outside of town where the sun was going down.
I remember the figures on the doors,
                            and the nails that held them there.

19

The needle, though it has clothed many, remains naked,
The proverb goes.
                    So with the spirit,
Silver as is the air silver, color of sunlight.
And stitches outside the body a garment of mist,
Tensile, invisible, unmovable, unceasing.

10

The Holston, past Rotherwood,
                          clear white and powder white,
The hills dark jade and light jade,
All of it flowing southwest
                    against the wind and the wind noise,

Summer enfrescoed in stop-time
                          alongside the Cumberlands,
Leo and Virgo slow as a cylinder turn overhead,
Wind in the trees, wind on the water.

11

Like clouds, once gone in their long drift,

                                    there's no coming back—

And like the wind that moves them, we stop
Wherever we please, or wherever we come to be,
Each one in his proper place,

                       not too near, not too far

From That's okay and No one was ever interested enough.

How many years have slipped through our hands?
At least as many as all the constellations we still can identify.
The quarter moon, like a light skiff,

                       floats out of the mist-remnants

Of last night's hard rain.
It, too, will slip through our fingers

                    with no ripple, without us in it.

How is it it's taken me almost a lifetime to come to the fact
That heaven and earth have no favorites

                    in either extreme?

Bits of us set out, at one time or another, in both directions,
Sleeping fitfully, heads on our fists,
Now close together and warm, now cold in the south sky.

Each one arrives in his own fashion,

                      each one with his birthmark

Beginning to take shape and shine out
And lead forth like a lead lamp.
Look for us in the black spaces, somewhere in the outer dark.

Look for us under the dead grass
                                in winter, elsewhere, self-satisfied, apart.

———————

A good writer is like a wind over meadow grass.
He bends the words to his will,
But is invisible everywhere.
Lament is strong in the bare places.
Among the winter trees, his words are fixed to music.

Or so we flatter ourselves,
                                sunset cloud tufts briquettes
Going ash in the ash-going sky.
We never look hard enough.
The grasses go back and forth, up and down, for thousands of miles,
But we don't look hard enough.

———————

Every other building a church,
Each side of the road,
                                Orebank half a mile long
Under the hill until the last curve
Down to the highway, left to Kingsport, right to Bristol,
East toward the rising sun, west toward home.

"Through the years of dust and sand," Tao-chi lamented,
Meaning his worldly ambitions
                                —his "single unworthy thought"
That set him adrift on the floating world—
                                his old age
Just recompense for what was not found,
Awaiting the great wash, a "final crash of thunder."

For half a lifetime, and more,

                               his days were the days of an ant,

His life, he thought, no longer than that of an insect

Going north on land,

                        going south on the raw rivers,

His last painting a single narcissus plant, his thoughts,

He wrote down, still wandering "beyond the boundless shores."

12

Water, apparently, is incomprehensible
At its beginning and at its end,
                              nothing into nothing,
And in between it's unsizable.
Certainly childhood water's that way,
The rivers coming from nowhere and going nowhere,
The lakes with no stopping place.
The waters of childhood are unimaginable.
The French Broad and Little Pigeon Rivers, the Holston,
Hiwassee and Cherokee Lakes,
                              Pickwick and Indian Path.
Water's immeasurable.

The heart is immeasurable,
                              and memory too.
Such little boxes to keep them in.
Like blue herons in heaven's field, they lift their long legs
Silently, and very slow,
In the ponds and back eddies they stalk through and rise from,
Air-colored in the sky-colored air.
How like the two of them to resettle then,
                              one hunting, one perched above.
Memory is a lonely observer,
                              the heart has thin legs.
They live in an infinite otherness, on dark snags,
In waters the color that they are,
                              and air is, the hard, endless air.

Snow, then sleet over snow, then snow again,

                                          the footprints still firm

Into the dark beyond the light's fall.

Whiter inside the darkness to the south than the north.

Whatever has been will be again

                            in the mind, in the world's flow,

Invisible armies outside the windows in rank,

Footprints continuing into the vestibules of the end.

———————

The light that shines forth from the emptiness does not sink,

They'd have you believe.

                       As well as whatever is next to it,

They'd also have you believe.

Philosopher, they are not able, philosopher.

And her begot him, think that.

———————

It's Groundhog Day, and sunlight is everywhere. Thank God.

Winter is such a comforting

                      with its sleet and icy dreams.

Shadows abound, and raw twigs,

The sharp edge of the absolute still snug in its loamy bed,

The template of its wings like shadows across the grass.

What poverty the heat of noon is,

And how we embrace it hard in our dutiful duds.

Short February.

How we will miss you and the actual world,

                               the singular,

The frozen composition that pentimentos our sorrow.

Still, for the time being, we have the sunlight that eats away
At our joy,
                    and still give thanks for that.
We try to count up the buttons on its golden coat,
But our eyes are unworthy.
We offer both our hands,
                              but they are unworthy too.

And so we remain transfixed
                              —the flowers from Delos
Unpurpled and stiff in their tarnished and silver bowl—
By sunlight,
Hoping the darkness will clear things up,
Hoping that what its handkerchief uncovers is what we get.

———————————

Just east of midnight,
                    the north sky scrolls from right to left,
A dark player piano.
No stopping the music, east to west,
                              no stopping it.

13

The small lights wander among the vacant trees like ghosts,
Whose roots have no voice in their deep sleep,
These lights that have no warmth in their drugged walk,

                damp flames and feckless.

The stars drift like cold fires through the watery roots of heaven,
These stars that are floating plants.
The small lights are not like that,

                but once were, I guess, light as a shadow.

What bodies will gather the lights in,

                or the stars in?
What waters will float their anxious rest?
Altar of darkness, altar of light, which tide will take them in?

14

The great mouth of the west hangs open,
                                    mountain incisors beginning to bite
Into the pink flesh of the sundown.
The end of another day
                    in this floating dream of a life.
Renown is a mouthful, here and there.

Rivers and mountains glide through my blood.
Cold pillow, bittersweet years.
In the near distance, a plane's drone
                                    rattles the windows.
Clear night. Wind like a predator
                            in the sharp grass of the past.

I find it much simpler now to see
                            the other side of my own death.
It wasn't always that way,
When the rivers were rivers and mountains were mountains.
Now, when the mouth closes,
                        the wind goes out of everything.

———————

Fame for a hundred years
                    is merely an afterlife,
And no friend of ours.
Better to watch the rain fall in the branches of winter trees.
Better to have your mail sent
To someone else in another town,
                            where frost is whiter than moonlight.

Horses, black horses:
                    Midnight, Five Minutes to Midnight.
Rider up, the sparks from their hooves like stars, like spiked stars.
This is a metaphor for failure,
This is the Rest of It, the beautiful horse, black horse.
Midnight. Dark horse, dark rider.

———————

I love the lethargy of the single cloud,
                                        the stillness of the sky
On winter afternoons, late on winter afternoons,
A little fan of light on the tips of the white pines.

I love the winter light, so thin, so unbuttery,
Transparent as plastic wrap
Clinging so effortlessly
                        to whatever it skins over.

—The language of nature, we know, is mathematics.
The language of landscape is language,
Metaphor, metaphor, metaphor,
                        all down the line.

The sweet-breath baby light of a winter afternoon,
Boy-light, half-covered in blue,
                        almost invisible as breath,
So still in the flower beds, so pale.

———————

Four days till the full moon,
                        light like a new skin on the dark
Quarter, like light unborrowed, hard,
                        black hole with its golden floor.

Who knows the happiness of fish,
                              their wind-raising, ordinary subtleties?
Describing the indescribable,
Image into idea,
                    the transmission of the spirit,
It cannot be done.

The Chinese principle, *breath-resonance-life-motion,*
Engenders, it was believed.
As does the bone method of brushwork,
Creating structure
                    in poems as well as pictures.

Plotting in paint, place in poetry,
Completes composition,
                         the bedrock of spiritual values.
Competent, marvelous, and *divine*
Were the three degrees of accomplishment.
                                    And still, it cannot be done.

Image resists all transmutation.
All art is meta-art, and has its own satisfactions.
But it's not divine,
                    as image is,
Untouchable, untransmutable,
                              wholly magic.

———————

Midnight Special, turn your ever-loving light on me.

15

You still love the ones you loved

                          back when you loved them—books,
Records, and people.
Nothing much changes in the glittering rooms of the heart,
Only the dark spaces half-reclaimed.

                        And then not much,
An image, a line. Sometimes a song.

Car doors slam, and slam again, next door.
Snow nibbles away at the edges of the dark ground.
The sudden memory of fur coats,

                        erotic and pungent,
On college girls in the backseats of cars, at Christmas,
Bourgeois America, the middle 1950s,

                        Appalachia downtown.

And where were we going? Nowhere.
Someone's house, the club, a movie?

                        See the pyramids along the Nile,
WKPT, *I'm itching like a man on a fuzzy tree.*
It didn't matter.
Martin Karant was spinning them out,

                        and the fur was so soft.

16

March is our master, the louche month we cannot control.
It passes like a river over us
—Cold current, warm spot—
                                        whose destination is always downstream,
Out of sight.
White water, easy water,
                                        March is a river over us.

Snow slam and sun burst,
                                        dead grass like peroxided hair
Unkempt among scattershot.
In Knoxville, across the street from James Agee's ex-house,
A small tree in full blossom,
Everything else still underground,
                                        river dark overhead.

I used to live here myself
                                        some sixty-five years ago.
Not here, precisely, but in the town,
Across town,
In a small house off the Kingston Pike,
No blossoming fruit limbs, no stripped, deciduous trees.

Love of the lack of love is still love
                                        wherever you find it,
I once heard an old man say,
In March, when the wind was westerly
                                        and the white clouds white as petals.
In March, in a vacant lot

On Chambliss Avenue, off the Kingston Pike.

And he was right.

I think I'm going to take my time,

life is too short

For immortality and its attendant disregards.
I have enough memories now for any weather,
Either here or there.

I'll take my time.

Tomorrow's not what I'm looking forward to, or the next day.
My home isn't here, but I doubt that it's there either—
Empty and full have the same glass,

though neither shows you the way.

Born again by water into the life of the spirit,

but not into the Life,

Rivers and lakes were my bread and wine,
Creeks were my transubstantiation.

And everything's holy by now,

Vole crawl and raven flyby,
All of the little incidents that sprinkle across the earth.

Easy enough to say,

but hard to live by and palliate.

Camus said that life is the search for the way back
To the few great simple truths
We knew at the beginning.
Out of the water, out to the cold air, that seems about right.

The moon, over Susan's house,

gobba a ponente,

34

Heading west toward the western reaches.
Snow-strikes streak my hair.

                                  We are all leaves in the current.

17

Leaning on Jesus, leaning on Jesus,

                                  leaning on the everlasting love.

That's a tough lean, Hernando,

When all the hackles of spring are raised,

                                  and its teeth glint

Like flint points in the sunshine,

Bright snarls from the underground.

Not much to lean on wherever you look,

                                above or below.

I remember my father in the spring,

                            who leaned on no one

And nothing, inspecting the rose plants

And the crusty, winter-warped mulch beds,

The blue distances over his back, over Cumberland Gap,

Opening like a great eye,

Jesus, he'd always say, Jesus, it's gone and done it again.

In Giorgio Morandi's bedroom and studio, it was always spring.

He would say, "Each time we begin,

                            we think we have understood,

That we have all the answers.

But it turns out we're just starting over again from the beginning."

Some bottles, a bed, and three tables,

The flowers abounding in little rectangles

                                all over the walls.

Meanwhile, in New York City,

Branch limbs scrubbed bare by winter;

                                         tiny fuses bumped at each end

Wait for Persephone's match.

———————

Spring freeze, and tulips cover their heads

                                        with iridescent hands;

Robins head for the hedges.
Even the insects back down
And cower inside their hiding holes.
Only the leaves seem cool, the new leaves,
Just butting their arrowed heads into the unforgiving blue.
How many lives these little ones lead.

                                  I wish that one of them were mine.

———————

A recluse should avoid the absolute,

                                  and its hills.

Master of words, Lord of signs, you've left me, where are you?
Down by the muddy waters, feeding the brilliant birds?
Half-returned, half still going away?
Now that you've gone,

                     I remember we've had an appointment there for years.

Don't move, I'm on my way.

It's quiet, no words, no words.
Is this just a silence, or just the start of the end?
Show yourself, Lord,

                     Master of What Is About to Be.

Stars turn brown in the river.
We share no happiness here—
Step out of the Out,

                     uncover your tongue and give me the protocol.

I'm starting to feel like an old man
                                                  alone in a small boat
In a snowfall of blossoms,
Only the south wind for company,
Drifting downriver, the beautiful costumes of spring
Approaching me down the runway
                                                of all I've ever wished for.

Voices from long ago floating across the water.
How to account for
                                     my single obsession about the past?
How to account for
                                     these blossoms as white as an autumn frost?
Dust of the future baptizing our faithless foreheads.
Alone in a small boat, released in a snowfall of blossoms.

Don't forget me little darling when they lay me down to die.
Just this one wish little darling that I pray.
As you linger there in sadness you are thinking of the past,
Let your teardrops kiss the flowers on my grave.

18

It's been, say, five years since I've been back here at this hour,
Evening starting its light-curling plane
                                        under the clouds,
The east-shrugged, flamingo clouds,
Everything different now, and everything just the same.
Except the leaves and birds,
                            great-grandchildren, and great-great.

It's not tomorrow I'm looking forward to, it's yesterday,
Or, better yet, the day before that.
The wind keeps gossiping in both my ears for nothing.
I can't go back there,
No matter how juicy the stories are,
                                    no matter how true, or untrue.

We don't know much, really, but we do know some things.
We know the people we learned from,
                                    and know what we learned.
We have to be humble about that—
I know what I got, and I know where I got it from,
Their names inscribed in my Book of Light.

All the while we thought we were writing for the angels,
And find, after all these years,
Our lines were written in black ink on the midnight sky,
Messages for the wind,
                        a flutter of billets-doux
From one dark heart to the next.

Who knew it would take so many years to realize
—Seventy years—that everything's light—
The day in its disappearing, the night sky in its distance, false dawn,
The waters that rise beneath the earth,
Bat wings and shadow pools,

                        that all things come from splendor?

The cardinal in his fiery caul,
The year's first dandelion globe,

                        ash-grey on the ash-green lawn,
Dear tulip leaves, color of carp bellies, wisteria drools
Withered and drained dry—
All light in the gathering darkness,

                        a brilliance itself which is set to come.

The cloud poets of ancient China
Saw what they saw and recorded it,

                        diviners of what wasn't there,
Prestidigitators of nothingness.

                    Let me be one of them.

Sun over plum-colored leaf planes,

                        shadows at ease in the east-going ivy.
A little wind, like a falling wind,
Tickles the planes, and they rise and fall.
Mid-May in the city garden,

                    sunlight in designated spaces
Among the buildings, golden for us, dun-dust next door,
The sun like the Green Knight's head,
Rolling in slow motion toward its distant and dark corner,
Bright drops on the bright green hedge,

                    black on the black borders.

In an opposite corner, splotches of sun and shade,
Like birthmarks all of us have,
Some on our faces, some on our hearts,
                                  all of them afterprints of our ruin,
Through which we step each morning
Gingerly, some of us going east, some of us going west.

19

This is the bird hour, peony blossoms falling bigger than wren hearts
On the cutting border's railroad ties,
Sparrows and other feathery things
Homing from one hedge to the next,

                     late May, gnat-floating evening.

Is love stronger than unlove?

                  Only the unloved know.
And the mockingbird, whose heart is cloned and colorless.

And who's this tiny chirper,

             lost in the loose leaves of the weeping cherry tree?
His song is not more than three feet off the ground, and singular,
And going nowhere.
Listen. It sounds a lot like you, hermano.

                    It sounds like me.

20

Don't sew the skins of land and sea animals
                                     into the same garment.
Over each grave, build a wooden house.
Burn children's toys to bring good weather.

And so on, the legends say.
                    Herons in mid-June stand up to their knees
In creek water, their wings like vinyl siding against their sides.
Next month they'll do the same thing.

Outside the cycle of seasons,
                    our lives appear meaningless,
No lilacs, no horse in the field, no heart-hurt, no sleeve:
Where time is constant and circular, all ends must meet.

———————

White clouds now dissipating in evening's turnaround,
No sound but the sound of no sound,
                              late sunlight falling on grass.

———————

A little knowledge of landscape whets isolation.
This is a country of water,
                    of water and rigid trees
That flank it and fall beneath its weight.
They lie like stricken ministers, grey and unredeemed.
The weight of water's unbearable,
                              and passes no judgment.
Side by side they lie, in intricate separation.

This is a country of deep inclemency, of strict
Self-immolation and strict return.
This is the way of the absolute,
                            dead grass and waste
Of water, clouds where it all begins, clouds where it ends,
Candle-point upshoots on all the upstart evergreens,
Sun behind west ridge,
                    no moon to sickle and shine through.

———————

Much is unknown up here,
                        much more still left to be unexplained.
Under the pines there's not much to see,
White clouds and grey clouds,
The shadows they carry inside themselves unto the world's end.
That sort of business. It's hard.

There are fourteen cliff swallow round-mouthed mud nests
                                            under the roof
Of the old barn house.
I stand and watch birds flying frantically after the rain,
Gold-breasted in the suddenly appearing sunlight.
Out of each hole a beak's unlevered.

Wang Wei had something to say about the unknowing:
Unable to throw off my remnant habits
I find the world has come to know me for them
My name and style—these they have right
But this heart of mine they still do not know.

———————

Morning, a small rain on the cabin,
                            cloud tears like blown fire smoke
Under the slow overcast.
Nothing to do but watch the larch boughs,

44

Color, almost, of my shirt,
                    flourish their crystal studs.

What is the span of one's life?
How do you measure it
                    before it goes back to formlessness?
This is of some note to the white-haired.
Cubits or years, missed opportunities,
                              the minor, self-satisfied
Successes that came, as all things must, down to nothing,
The time it took to get there?

There is a resignation in all things deep as dirt,
A knowledge that no one lacks,
A force that finds its way
                    to the tip of every thing.
There is a serenity
Under our layers that rocks like a cradle of calm waters.
There is a freshness that we abide.

Deer huddle like cattle around the salt block,
                              then burst like flames in the air.
The white clouds slide from the south
Like an edge of ice.
The swallows harangue and arabesque
Over the lawn and lilac rim of the late lilacs,
Then dwindle against the dark green of the evergreens.

Last bird call, sun disappearing
                    under the right edge of things.
All that I know goes with it,
Isolate, like a body pulled down by weights
                              into the depths.

21

At seventy, it's always evening,
                              light diluted,
Breeze like a limp hand
Just stirring the long-haired grasses, then letting them be.
The dark decade, beginning its long descent
                                        out over the blank Atlantic,
Against the wind, inexorable,
The light dissolving like distance in the evergreens.
Even the clouds find a place to rest.

And that's the way it should be,
Swallows swarming like gnats
                              in the gnat-infested air,
Tree shadows lying like limbed logs across the meadow,
Slowly sinking into the hill's shadow that stalks them.
Deer raise their white flags and leave the field,
The sapsucker leaves her nest
In the barn house wall,
                    and everything moves toward its self-appointed end.

I keep on thinking,
                    If I sit here for long enough,
A line, one true line,
Will rise like some miraculous fish to the surface,
Brilliant and lithe in the late sunlight,
And offer itself into my hands.
I keep thinking that as the weeks go by,
                                        and the waters never change.
I keep thinking that as the sun goes down and the birds fly home.

The sky is cloudless, the meadow seems like a vast plain
Without dust,
                the Chinese vocabulary of the grasses
Shining like water wherever I dip my dark brush.
I have loved, and been loved in return, by solitude.
Back fifty feet in the pines,
All color relents,
And the quietness there, the stern quietness,
                                is hard as stone.

————————

At my age, memories scatter like rain
                        when one sits still, first day of summer,
The noise of the world
                over a hundred miles away,
Sun sinking, but not as soon as yesterday, birds flown.

————————

What does one do when you find out your thoughts
                        are the thoughts of everyone else?
Wait for a monk to come down
From his hill,
Look hard for the people whose lives you cannot explain,
Walk slowly under the shagbark trees?
I can't know, but as one ages
                it comes as a matter of some reflection.

There are worse desolations, of course.
                Abandoned cities, for one thing,
The thousand miles that stretch out
From one image to the next.
We all hum our own sad songs.
Make yours your favorite, and don't look
At the new grass, at the summer sun
                        in its dangling descent.

———————

Light falls on the deer and the jump weed,
Light out my west window,
                              June light, the Sundown Special.
We know where she's headed—
                              your seat is used, but reserved.

———————

This is the entry of evening light.
Where I am, it seems, it's always just before sunset.
At least nowadays,
Even in memory—
                    Lake Garda and Mykonos,
Venice, of course, and every place one can stand
                                        upon the abiding earth.
Local color still deep in the heart.
O my, as I said one time, I love to see that evening sun go down.

All the little black bugs have left the dandelions,
The robins have gone.
Even the clouds have changed
                          to the color of 2% milk.
Out the north window, the grasses stand bright and erect as acolytes.
I remember the way they stood at Desenzano, like that,
Some forty-five years ago,
Though I didn't pay much attention then,
                              twenty-three, on my way to anywhere else.

We're always, apparently, on our way to anywhere else,
And miss what we're here for,
                          the objects we never realize
Will constitute our desire,
The outtakes and throwaways of the natural world.
The movement of creek water at dusk,

The slippage and slow disappearance of what we love
Into the silence of here-and-now
                              that will survive us, and call back.

———————

The barn house is upside down in the motionless pond.
And pine trees.
                Two ducks land suddenly
And everything's carried away in blurred, colorful pieces.

22

The summer passing of the black-sailed familiar,
The ghost bier of the Hunter Gracchus,

                              myth-driven, ill at ease,

Two-masted and low, is now at hand.
A wrong turn, a lack of attention,

                          a lack, it seems, of love,

Has set its last course.
Like the four seasons, it wheels on the rings of air forever.

When the body is old, the heart becomes older still.

23

One needs no Paradise when the rain falls,
                            and clouds are not scattered by the wind.
No one's around, the grasses bend at their belt buckles,
Boughs droop and the rain keeps coming down.
There is an edgy serenity in solitude,
                            when the rain falls and the wind stops,
The perpetual presence of absence, where all things are still.

Rain over everything like sunlight,
                            out of the clouds.
Shining in strings and beads, a giant hush,
Like tongues in the afterlife.
Clouds like the smoky aftereffect of forest fires,
High-drift and hang.
                    Out of the stillness, a small splendor.

————————

The line between heaven and earth is a grass blade,
                            a light green and hard to walk.

————————

Bigfoot, the north wind, slaps through the trees
Looking for something that we can't know,
                            or even, perhaps, have heard of,
Pushing the boughs aside,
                    always gone, just out of sight.
Sunlight fills in his footprints.

After the answer, there's always another question,

Even the last one.
>   At least we have that to count on.
I am an image picker.
I like the ripe ones,
>   the ones at the ends of the listing limbs.

To know one's self is the final yes, of course.
>   The no,
However, is right behind it, and just as final.
How easy to lose oneself in the orchard,
>   this tree and that,
Everything shiny, everything slick and close to hand.

———————

The evening prepares for the invisible,
>   the absence of itself.
Clouds defuse. White cat on the fence pole
Haunched on her throne.
>   Bird feathers glued to the window glass
Where finch attempted his noon flight through the visible.
Better to keep your head down,
>   asleep in the darkening trees.
Nothing can stop it. One sweep of its cape and it's gone.

———————

The morning is almost silent and cannot declare itself.
Therefore, I say unto it,
>   you are the never-boring miracle
Of sunlight and scrappy cloud,
The absence of rain when rain is absent,
>   as it is
This morning, green with its wonderment,
Last night's hard frost a wet memory
Scattered in bits and glitzy pieces
>   deep in the grass.

The ten horses of the field are like
                              the cities of the plain,
A necessary moment
Of everything that is, and was, and will be again,
Standing in succulence in the brevity of time.
The sunlight grows big,
                    immensity
Of noon approaching, its spurs flashing and its saber on fire.
The green backs off a bit, and mumbles. And so do we.

——————

I have nothing to say. I am a recording machine,
                              a listening device.
What I hear is what I will tell you.

I am the sluice of dead scrolls and songs,
                              I am the tongue of what exists,
Whose secrets are whispered and not heard.
Listen to me, listen to what's the nothing I have to say.

——————

The shadows of the floating world
                              huddle beneath their objects.
Slowly, like hands on a massive clock,
They soon will begin their crawl and creep
                              to bring us back
Tick-tock in their black sack, tick-tock in their soft black sack.

——————

Lord of the sunlight,
                Lord of the leftover, Lord of the yet-to-do,
Handle my heaven-lack, hold my hand.

24

The little birds are honing their beaks on the chopping block stump.
The clouds have gathered for their convention
                                from deep out in the dark Pacific.
They clear their throats and speak out.
Everything stills and listens,
                                even the little birds
With their sharp beaks and sharp claws,
                                        clinging inside the tamaracks
Until the storm passes and the cloud bodies adjourn.

That's when the big birds come,
                                with their sweeping wings and dangling legs,
Their eyes ajar, and the lightning sparks from their keening claws.
The poppies along the near hill glisten like small fires,
Pink and orange and damp red.
Behind the glass window, we hear the swoosh of the giant wings,
And listen hard for the next pass,
                                but they don't come back.

It's not such a poverty, we think,
                                to live in a metaphysical world.
Thus we become poor, and spurn the riches of the earth.
Such nonsense.
The crow flies with his beak open,
                                emitting a raucous cry.
The yearling horses stand in the field,
                                up to their knees in the new grass.
This is the first world we live in, there is no second.

The mind's the affliction,

                         asleep for a hundred years,

Nothing to wake it but memory,

The deep blank of memory,

                         rivers and hills, the morning sun,

Simple things,

               the body moving, not much, but moving.

Orpheus walked, the poets say, down to the black river.

Nobody recognized him,

Of course, and the boat came,

                         the gondola with its singular oarsman,

And the crowd got in, a thousand souls,

So light that the boat drew no water, not even a half inch.

On the other side, the one paved road, and they took it.

Afterward, echoes of the great song webbed in their ears,

They took the same road back to the waiting gondola,

The two of them,

               the first to have ever returned to the soot-free shore.

The oarsman's stroke never faltered, and he hummed the song

He had caught the faint edges of

                         from the distant, marble halls.

It won't work, he thought to himself, it won't work. And it didn't.

Clouds, like the hills of heaven,

Are nowhere in evidence tonight.

                         Sundown, an empty sky.

Except for the quarter moon, like a sail with no ship,

And no home port to come to.

                       Its world is without end.

The smallest cloud I've ever seen
                                floats like a white midge
Over the western ridgeline,
Then vanishes in the wind and the dying sunlight.
How unremarkable,
                        though no moon comes to shine on its going out.
And nothing arrives to take its place.
Forlorn evening, that makes me want to sit here forever, and then
        some.
I'll likely meet it again, a thousand years from now,
When it rises up through my bedroom,
                                buzzing against the windowpane.

———————

We are the generations of the soil,
                                it is our cloak and put-on.
Somnambulistas of sore intent,
Barefoot or full-shod, it is our destination,
                                our Compostela.
We rub its rock for luck, and slip inside to get warm,
As though, like our grandfathers before us,
                                we lie down in our own hearts.

———————

The dogs are barking under the newly planted trees.
When we're transplanted, they'll bark again,
                                but not for us.

25

I never tire of watching the mists rise
                              under the mountain
After the rain, like a small detail
On a Chinese screen.
                    The overcast, usually,
Is starting to break, like this evening,
Into its horizontal whites and greys and scrimmed blues.
The mists invisibly come together and dissipate, come
Together and dissipate.
I never get tired of watching this,
As the mists seem to move, then not move.
They don't, of course, but merely disappear.
                                   Perhaps that's why I like it.
The light is flat and hard and almost nonexistent,
The way our lives appear to us,
                         then don't, as our inlook shifts.
The horses know nothing of any of this, their heads in the wet grass.
And you know nothing of this, asleep, as you are, in the distant field.
Asleep, as you always will be, in the distant field.

———————

I've always loved, as Auden called them, the chinks in the forest,
(He had the deer peer through them)
Those little slashes and blades
                         of sunlight cutting streaks
Between the trees, imperceptibly healing over
As sunset pulls back down its high road
And the dark bandages of dusk
                         are placed on the forest floor.

I love to watch them thrust and retreat,

                                blazing the trees,

Making a trail so full of light that no one can follow it.

———————

I've looked at this landscape long enough,

                                time for another book.

One less endless, perhaps, a finitude to count on

And not this enduring verdancy

And chapterless blue.

Sometimes one feels the need of ordinary things,

                                flies

Carcasses along the windowsills, wasps

Resurgent under the eaves,

Dropped feathers, pine chips.

                        Sometimes you've got to face the dog.

———————

Just after the war (the Second World War), in Kingsport,

I started listening to music,

Local music, east Tennessee and southwest Virginia,

"Rock of Ages," "The Great Speckled Bird," "Life Is Like a Mountain
    Railroad."

Like all children, I just accepted things,

                          and never puzzled them out.

But "The Great Speckled Bird" was a different lyric.

I never could quite imagine it,

Though the song never failed to move my feet to music.

The great wings shadowed my childhood,

                        and still do, from time to time,

Darkening some. Then darkening more.

There are songs, we now know, to be sung on the other side of
    language.
Our tongues are not capable, however,
                our eyes can't trill in the dark.

Sometimes I feel I've already told
            every story I've ever heard,
Or even once heard about.
God knows, even those are short enough,
And not, in their narratives, deliciously slow and drawn out.
I think, I guess, that immanence isn't a story,
And can't be.
        In truth, it isn't linguistic at all,
Or metalinguistic either, or any of that.
So stub out your pencil, Pilgrim,
           and listen to what the wind repeats
As it starts and erases itself,
Unstoppable storyteller with nothing to say.
I'd like to cry out in its book,
          especially when it stalls,
On that blank page between one narrative and the next.

In the darkness between the tamaracks,
         the light is bundled like little sticks,
Like fatwood for the fire about to start with the evening's match.

26

A word to the wise is a word to the wise,

                         and isn't sufficient

To anything in this world.

Give me a thing that says nothing.

                            The wind, for instance,

A wisdom that comes from ten thousand miles to the west.

The trees, for instance, stenographers

Of every sentence it isn't able to utter.

The grass that assembles them all

                        in its green pages.

The dirt that subtracts each word, syllable after syllable,

Into its dark book, and keeps them there

In ignorance, a blessed ignorance we'll come to know,

A radiant cloud at our mouths,

                      breath like no other.

Whoever would lay a seed of truth on the table

Had best have his left foot in the stirrup

                      and both hands

On the saddle, and be good to go.

The wise is without wisdom, and that's as it should be,

So many words, so many.

The truth is another matter, and is, like wisdom,

As speechless as bull clover.

Outside, in the sun, Yugo the dog lies quietly,

His head on his paws.

What he sees he can't say,

                  but he sees what you see and I see.

His look is pure and pitiless and not on the what's-to-come.

The little finches have come and gone
                                    back to their tree.
They lay these words on my eyelids, grains of sleep.
                            Look for me, witness, look for me.

The one-legged metal-green rooster
Nailed to the wall of the old chicken house
                                    is all that remains
Of Snuffy Bruns, at least in these parts.
A small wooden platform where Beryl, his wife (his sister
As well, it turned out), would feed Marcia,
A pine squirrel she'd almost domesticated,
                                    who would come when called,
Rots on a spruce tree by the outhouse.
He called me Easy Money—I liked that—and made the best knives
You're likely to come across.
Of the two, he died first, and early, much liked by all of us.
And Beryl was taken in downriver
By some family we didn't know well.
They came from Colorado, I think.
I loved his toothless grin and his laid-back ways.
                                    They shipped him there,
Careful truck driver to the end, after the last handshake and air-kiss,
From one big set of mountains to another, in a slow rig.

Tonight the ravens are dominant,
                                    and whoosh the air
With their wings like oars on a black boat.
Who's dead, who's dead, they croak,
                                    going from tree to tree limb,
Five of them, six of them, looking for blood and a place to land.

Not me, I mutter, not me.
Four ducks take off in loose formation like fighter planes.
Not them either, apparently.
                              So long, ducks, so long,
Ravens resting a moment above the pond,
                                        and then they're gone,
The evening as still and tranquil as the inside of a bone
Till they return. And return they will,
Looking for what's available and warm, and what's not.
We live in their shadow, and under it,
                                    and our days are long.

————————

Don't sit by the side door, waiting for hangnail and radiance,
The past is a yellow dust.

Do what the wind does,
And let your life be heavier: no darkness, no light.

————————

The birds keep flying into the windows.
                              They see the sky reflected
And keep on breaking their necks.
The birds keep flying into the windows.
                              They see the reflection of the sky.

27

The level's so low in the short pond,
The snipe seems to walk on water,
                                    ruffling his dagger-drawn wings
As he heads for the next mossed hillock.
Suddenly, under a cloud, the sun's bottom auras the pond's surface,
And snipe is consumed by fire,
                          still walking, angelic, wings dipped in flame.
It must have been like this on the first retelling, back there on the
     long water,
Such mystery,
     sunlight and surface-shine and something winged on the waves,
Snipe settled now, deep beak in the curls.

The logo is Fra Angelico,
                          alone in the unfinished rooms
Upstairs in S. Marco, blank windows
He colored with apparitions and visitations,
The outlines already there,
Apparently, waiting to be filled in.
                          And he filled them, stroke by stroke,
Bringing the outside inside.
He painted, it's been said, the first recognizable landscape.
As for the others,
               he gathered the form from the air, and gave it flesh.

———————

The snipe stands on top of himself
                          on the water beneath him.
When he drinks, he drinks from his own mouth.

What could be luckier, as full of grace and replenishment,
As feeding oneself on one's other self, one's stand-in,
Life's little helper swagged under our feet,
                                    one's doppelgänger and replica?

Windless, just-August evening.
Only the grasses move, and slightly,
The tall grasses, hearing the whispers of gravity,
And turning their tired necks
                        as though they'd prefer not to.
Otherwise, not even the stubbed clover moves, nor the snipe,
                                        either of them.

—————

August, blue mother, is calling her children in
                                soundlessly
Out of the sun-dried thistles
And out of the morning's dewlessness.
All of the little ones,
                the hard-backed and flimsy-winged,
The many-legged and short-of-breath,
She calls them all, and they come.

Listen, this time I think she's calling your name as well.

—————

I wish I remembered the way the stars looked
                            up here some thirty-five years ago
When the lights went out.
Pretty much as they do now, I'd guess,
Though I never see them,
                    given, as now I am, to an early bed.
Original oxymorons, ice on fire, I loved to watch them fall.

And loved them, too, as they stayed in place,
Designs from the afterlife of dreams,
                              and beyond that,
Connecting the dots of nothingness.
It comforts me to know they're up there,
                              and that their light
Keeps coming long after my sleep has gone forth, and my sleep's sleep.

———————

We've all lead raucous lives,
                              some of them inside, some of them out.
But only the poem you leave behind is what's important.
Everyone knows this.
The voyage into the interior is all that matters,
Whatever your ride.
Sometimes I can't sit still for all the asininities I read.
Give me the hummingbird, who has to eat sixty times
His own weight a day just to stay alive.
                              Now that's a life on the edge.

———————

I live here accompanied by clouds
Now that the weather's broken.
They take and release sunlight
                              like stained glass outside my small window.
A light that sometimes prompts me to want
To leave the world and settle, like some white bird,
                              on another mountain.

28

What does it profit us to say
The stiff new bristles of the spruce tree
Glisten like bottle brushes after the rain shower?
To what avail is the thunderstorm
Passing just north of us, and south too,
Like a growling and wire-haired dog
                              still wishing us harm?
Description and metaphor,
The fancy dancing of language,
                    to what good end, my friend, to what end?
And who will remember us and our enterprise,
Whose fingers will sift our dust?

We'll never know, Horatio, we will never know.

———————

Cold snap, not even mid-August yet,
The little engines of change at work
Unexpectedly in the atmosphere
                              as well as our lives,
The dragging, black-bellied clouds
That enter our blood from the wrong side of the compass,
The double-clutch of wind-shift
Into off-limits and unappeasable places
Is coming our way soon,
                    and slow-dropped out of the blue.
One sees it and feels it at the same time,
                                    noiselessly
Pulling toward the meridian, then over the hill.

The evening's homily comes down to this in the end:
Praise for the left-out and left-behind,
Praise for the left-over and over-looked,

                        praise for the left hand
And the horse with one lame leg,
Praise for the going-down,

                and the farther going-down,
Praise for the half-things, red moon and the smoke-scented sky,
The bling and the left half of the heart,
The half-winded whicker of geldings,

                      light water on top of the dark,
The dispossession of all landscape
As night cuts the music off,

              and pulls the plug and eases in.

The overheated vocabulary of the sun
Has sunk to just a few syllables,

              fewer than yesterday.
And fewer still tomorrow, I'd bet.
Slaphappy sidekick, guttering old fool,

                tongue-tied and toasty,
What are your last ones likely to be, "you"? Or will they be "the"?

Bringing the horses in is like

              bringing the past of the whole race in.
Sundown, a cloud-flittered sky.
They'd like blood, but hay is what they get,
Ghosts from our former lives,

              ghosts who could carry us still.
Breathe lightly into their nostrils, scorgle their muzzles.
They brought us here,

            and someday they'll take us far away.

———————

Twenty hours of rain in the middle of August,
No thunder, no lightning strikes.
A gift.
        I saw two kingfishers last week outside my window,
Above the creek. I hope they'll come back.
Autumn is under way, already the first gears

                                    notched and turned.

———————

Abandoned squirrel nest under cloud-slide.

                                    Pencil stub.
The dread of what we can see, and the dread of what we can't see,
Crawl in the same manner,

                        one in back of the other.

———————

Struck by the paucity of my imagination
To winnow the meadow from anything that it is,
I watch the yellow-tail hawk

                        cruising its edges, the willows
Along the creek's course,
Low down and lethal, then up like a slung lariat
To circle and telescope,
Eventually to noose back down
And crumble,

            only to rise, big wings pumping, back to the west.

Beside me, the shadow of the wind chime's bamboo drag
Turns like a fish on a string
Noiselessly in the still waters of morning's sunlight.
A pack train of white and off-white clouds
Works east where the hawk had been.

                        Almost noon, the meadow

Waiting for someone to change it into an other. Not me.
The horses, Monte and Littlefoot,
Like it the way it is.

                And this morning, so do I.

———————

After the end of something, there comes another end,
This one behind you, and far away.
Only a lifetime can get you to it,

                        and then just barely.

29

The page is dark, and the story line is darker still.
We all have the same book,

                              identically inscribed.
We open it at the appointed day, and begin to read.

30

There is a kind of depression that empties the soul.
The eyes stay bright,
                    the mind stays clear as Canada on an autumn day
Just after the rain.
But the soul hangs loose as a plastic bag in a tree
When the wind has died.
                    It is that drained.
And overcast. The little jack-weeds
That line its edges exhale,
And everything falls to a still, uneasy remove.
It stirs when the wind shifts,
                    and seasons tumble and stall.
It stirs, but it doesn't disappear.
Though weeds re-up and the clouds relent,
                    it doesn't disappear.

———————

Like a golden Afro, a bunch of eidergrass has blossomed
And paled out
On top of an uprooted pine stump
Across the creek.
                    As the sun goes down,
What small light there is drains off into its spikiness,
And glows like a severed head against the darkness.

———————

Oil lamp lit, outside light a similitude,
                    wet world

From recent downpour,

I think of you back in Massachusetts,

                                hurting from head to foot heel,
Still summer there, autumn beginning here, no drop of complaint.

Brushstroke, bullrushes in front of pond's mirror,

                                     rain spots
Pimpling diminished mountain.
My seventieth birthday,

                    such wonderful weather.

Whatever lights there are are ours, or can be,

                            all things
We see are like that.
And those we can't see gather the light

                            closely unto themselves,
And look around steadily for us.
How is it we miss their messages?

August the 25th, the snipe gone.

                        Do they go south?
I suppose they must, but where?
Certainly not to east Tennessee,
Where I held the bag for hours

                        in Oak Ridge one evening after supper
(There goes the kingfisher, and then the yellow-tail hawk,
One up the creek, the other one down).
I hope they are walking now on a warmer water,
And that their reflections are just as clear,

                            and the moss as green.
Sixty-two years ago, the year of aluminum pennies,
My hands still burning,

                  the mouth of that croker sack still open.

Lord, when the world is still, how still it is,

                                    contrails and mare's tails
Crisscrossing the sky,
Patterned so lightly on its unmistakable air.
One waits for a presence from the darkening woods,

                                    one large and undiminished,
But only its absence appears, big as all get-out.

Evening arrives so swiftly these days

                                    even the weak-kneed weeds
Don't know which direction to bow in,
The fugitive wind-fingers,
Groping north, groping south,

                              then hanging like unstruck chimes
From their disused and desolate hands.

Out over the sunlit Pacific
Mischief is in the making

                              (Good, there's the kingfisher again,
Then gone in a blue, acetylene flash
Down to the trout horde),
Whose scratches and plum knots

                              we'll feel in a day or two.

————————

The world's whinny and the world's bit

                              are two thousand miles away.
How is it I hear its hoofbeats so sharp in my ear?

31

Emptiness happens.
                  It's like the down-curving dead branch
On the pine tree outside my window
Which ends in nothing, its mossy beard
Moving just slightly, no more than that, in the slight wind.
One hopes, in due time, to be so moved,
                            in just such a garment.

There's an easy emptiness, and a hard emptiness,
The first one knowable, the second one not,
                      though some are said to have seen it
And come back to fight the first.
Which is bespoke, and fits like a shirt.
The second one's colorless, and far away,
                           as love is, or a resurrection.

The bottles my messages are sent in have long disappeared.
Cloudy September jumbles the sky.
The great purity waits for me,
                      but no one has answered my questions.

These are the night journals,
                      an almanac of the afterhour,
Icarus having fallen
A long time ago, the sun in its ghostly pursuit
Behind him behind the ridge,
Not enough light to see the page,

                              not really,
Much less to imagine how it must have been, the pale boy
Scalded by burning wax,
                              cooled by wind,
The water a sudden oblivion, so nothing, so welcoming,
So many worlds since then, all of them so alike, all of them
Suncatcher, father and son.

                    ——————

The beginning of autumn dark is quick, and it's cold, and long.
My time of life is a preen of feathers, and goes on and on.
If not in me, then in you,
                              cousin.
I'll look for you in the deep light, on the other side.
The water is wadable,
                    not too big, not too small.
I'll be the one with white hair, avoiding the mirror.

                    ——————

It's odd how certain combinations
                         are carved twice in the memory,
Once in the surface riprap and once in the deep seams.
Lake Garda is like that, and Valpolicella wine,
The sun going down above Salò,
The waters, as has been said,
                         crumpling and smoothing toward Bardolino,
Fish on the grill, the wine like blood in liter carafes,
The dusk a darkish serenity laying its hands
On our shoulders
                    warmly, with a touch of freshness, but warmly.
When you're twenty-three, you'll live forever, a short time.

                    ——————

One horse up and one horse down.

                              And Punta S. Vigilio,
Olive trees semaphoring in the wind O love me.
And I did, I did.
                    I wonder if I will ever see it again?
And Riva, that myth-bag, Gardone,
And all the way over and back to Sirmione?
And Thorpe and Hobart and Schimmel and Schneeman,
                                        will I see them,
And Via Mazzini, La Greppia, Piazza Erbe?
Not as they were and not as I was.
The past is a dark disaster, and no one returns.
Initials are left, and dates.
Sometimes the bodies are still hanging,
                              and sometimes not.

                  ──────────

Hark, hark, the dogs do bark;
The poets are coming to town.
One in rags and one in tags,
And one in a silken gown.

32

Backyard, my old station, the dusk invisible in the trees,
But there in its stylish tint,
Everything etched and precise before the acid bath
—Hemlocks and hedgerows—
Of just about half an hour from now,
Night in its soak and dissolve.
Pipistrello, and gun of motorcycles downhill,
A flirt and a gritty punctuation to the day's demise
And one-starred exhalation,
                                        V of geese going south,
My mind in their backwash, going north.

———————

The old gospel song from 1950
                              by Lester Flatt and Earl Scruggs,
"Reunion in Heaven," has a fugitive last verse
I must have heard once
Although it wasn't included when they recorded it.
So I'll list it here,
                    that it won't be disremembered.
Just in case.
I am longing to sit by the banks of the river
There's rest for the ones by the evergreen trees
I am longing to look in the face of my Savior
And my loved ones who have gone, they are waiting for me

———————

When what you write about is what you see,
                              what do you write about when it's dark?

77

Paradise, Pound said, was real to Dante because he saw it.
Nothing invented.
One loves a story like that, whether it's true or not.
Whenever I open my eyes at night, outside,

                              flames edge at the edge
Of everything, like the sides of a nineteenth-century negative.
If time is a black dog, and it is,
Why do I always see its breath,

                       its orange, rectangular breath
In the dark?
It's what I see, you might say, it's got to be what my eyes see.

———————

So many joys in such a brief stay.
Life is a long walk on a short pier.

———————

If poetry is pentimento,

                   as most of its bones seem to show,
Remember the dead deer on Montana 92,
Lincoln County, last Monday, scrunched in the left-hand ditch.
Raven meat-squawks for two days.
On Thursday, south wind through the rib cage,
Ever-so-slightly a breathing,

                   skull-skink unmoved on the macadam.
Its song was somewhat, somewhat erased.

———————

I'm early, no one in the boat on the dark river.
It drifts across by itself
Below me.

             Offended, I turn back up the damp steps.

The dragonflies remain a great mystery to me.
Early October.
                    At least a dozen of them are swarming
Like swallows over the dying grass
And browned leaves of the backyard,
Each tending to recompose a previous flight path
With minor variations.
So beautiful,
                    translucent wings against the translucent sky,
The late afternoon like litmus just under our fingertips.

—————

The berries shine like little stigmata in the dogwood trees,
A thousand reminders of the tree's mythology
As the rain keeps polishing them,
                    as though it could rub it clean.

Such red, and Easter so far away.

33

The song of someone like me

                              begins on the pennywhistle.

A few notes, just a few, up and down.

The bass line comes in,

                      then the lead and second guitar.

Brushstrokes on the snares.

And then the singer, Lord, then the singer steps up.

What voice could slip this backdrop?

Only the rise and fall of the newly damned, perhaps,

                                 or the Great Speckled Bird.

Or some sough through the big larch limbs, some sibilance in the pines.

Little lost squawks in the natural world,

                             lost voices.

I gather them unto me, I become their mouthpiece.

Sordello, with lazy and honest eyes, still waits for us

Beyond the *palude* off Via Mantovana

Just this side of Sabbionetta,

His terraced, invisible mountain

Rising above Lake Garda into the infinite.

Not time for that hike yet, we hoped,

                            feet hot on the cobblestones

In front of Palazzo Ducale.

Not yet, we hoped, our foreheads already feeling the sword's tip.

And angel wings.

                 You got to carry that weight for a long time,

And pray for the angel's wing

When the time comes, when the time does come.

Moonlight like watery paint
On the yard grass and arborvitae.

Shadows like Franz Kline from the spruce trees.

Circle of neighbor's basketball goal like the entrance to Hell
On stone-spattered, leaf-littered driveway.

October, old ghost month, you outline my *fine del cammin.*

———

There is a photograph of Stan Hyman and me in our Army dress
      blues,
2nd Lieutenants, standing in front of a No Parking sign
In Pacific Grove, California, 1958.
There are a hundred million snapshots
Just like it, Stan's wedding day, the 24 August.
Mine means a world to me, a world never to return,
But one never left, if truth be told.
And yours? You have at least one, I know, just like it,
                    different people, different place,
But the same. What does it mean to you?
Who could imagine it would ever become like this?

———

All I have left undone, I hope someone will make good
In this life or the next,
               whichever comes first. Or second.

———

Moon riseth not, as some Victorian must have said back in the day,
Stars like a motorcycle's exhaust
Through the limp leaves of the maple trees.

Not much excitement here,
Though headlights and taillights go back and
Forth like pine-pitch torches in some Attic procession,
The limbs of Orpheus overhead
At the front,
            his blue-tongued and pale head behind on the slow Rivanna,
Bumping from snag to sandbar, but singing, still singing.

The start of things, and the end of things,
Two unmarked graves,
                        the autumn wind rising west of the mountains.
Goodbye to the promise of What's Left.

The emptiness of nonbeing,
                        that which endures through all change—
Something to shoot for, for sure,
Something to seek out and walk on,
                                    one footprint after the next.
In any case, after this life of who-knows-how-many-years,
Who's not a shrunken, pitiable sight?

I empty myself with light
Until I become morning.

34

It's dark now, but I remember the five-fingered jaundiced leaves
Seeming to hover above the earth this afternoon
On the tips, the dull tips, of grass blades
                              under the maple tree,
The dogwood berries on Locust Avenue like scarlet cluster bombs,
Automobiles and ambulance sirens
                              cutting the sundown, October air,
Thinking, this isn't at all bad, not even one bit,
All the way to the hospital, and all the way back.
And now here's Mars, like a pancake orange,
Northeast in the bleached-star sky,
                              and that's not at all bad either,
End of October, end of a buffed and edgeless day.

———————

Halloween, All Hallows' Eve.
                              And what if they came back,
All of them, what would we say?
That the moon looks good through the limbs of the chinaberry tree?
That the night air is as easy as oil on the skin?
That the children parading in their pathetic little costumes
                              have it right?
That the give in the natural world
Is as good as the take in the supernatural other?
That the moon looks good and the stars still refuse to shine?
What would we say, Slick, what would we say,
Our hands like skeletal party gloves,
                              our masks future faces?

I think of the masters of a century ago,
And often wish they'd come and whisper their secrets in my ear,
My right ear, the good one. Not all, perhaps, but a couple.

The fallen leaves
                        litter the lawn and driveway. Autumn.
Indian summer. Nothing ripples.
The other side of the world, they say, is a door
                        where I'll find my life again.

New moon like a jai alai basket
                        just over the doctor's rooftop,
Cradling the old moon before her fall.

If angels can see into the ends and beginnings of things,
Why are they still among us
Like widowed birds, circling, circling,
                        their poor go-betweens at a full stop?

The cold gowns of the masters,
                        those of a thousand years ago,
Over a thousand, and then some,
Wander the countryside,
                        brushing like loose crystal against the sumac.
Who here can inhabit them?
Whose arms among us can fill their sleeves,
So clear and transparent, so radiant in the dark?

My neighbor's maple tree shines like a galleon in the dusk,
Kumquat and blood orange,

               pomegranate and nectarine.
Within such splendor, everything falls away, even our names,
All trace of our being here, breathed in by the night's lips.
This is as close as we get to them,
Their tinkling crystal folds just ahead of us

                        how sweet a sound.

Is there an emptiness we all share?

                  Before the end, I mean.
Heaven and earth depend on this clarity,

                      heaven and earth.
Under the gold doubloons of the fallen maple leaves,
The underworld burrows in,

               sick to death of the light.

35

When death shall close these eyelids,
And this heart shall cease to beat,
And they lay me down to rest
In some flowery-bound retreat.

Will you miss me, will you miss me,
Will you miss me,
Will you miss me when I'm gone?

Perhaps you'll plant a flower
On my poor, unworthy grave,
Come and sit alone beside me
When the roses nod and wave.

Will you miss me, will you miss me,
Will you miss me,
Will you miss me when I'm gone?

One sweet thought my soul shall cherish
When this fleeting life has flown,
This sweet thought will cheer when dying,
Will you miss me when I'm gone?

When these lips shall never more
Press a kiss upon thy brow,
But lie cold and still in death,
Will you love me then as now?

Will you miss me, will you miss me,
Will you miss me,
Will you miss me when I'm gone?

Notes

2. *Nag Hammadi Library*, James M. Robinson, general editor, Harper & Row, 1978.

9. W. G. Sebald, "Dr. K. Takes the Waters at Riva," in *Vertigo*, New Directions, 1999.

10. For Wilma Hammond.

11. *Returning Home, Tao-Chi's Album of Landscapes and Flowers*, introduction and commentaries by Wen Fong, George Braziller, 1976.

17. *Mountain Home*, translated by David Hinton, Counterpoint, 2002.

18. Ryan Fox, Sonny Rollins.

20. Elizabeth Kolbert, *The New Yorker*, June 2005.

20. *Poems of Wang Wei*, translated by G. W. Robinson, Penguin Classics, 1973.

23. *The Collected Poems of Wallace Stevens*, Knopf, 1954.

33. Giuseppe Ungaretti, "Mattino."

34. Bob Dylan, "It Takes a Lot to Laugh, It Takes a Train to Cry."

35. A. P. Carter, "Will You Miss Me When I'm Gone."